COOL BRANDS

Jillian Powell

Editorial Consultant – Cliff Moon

RISING★STARS

nasen
NASEN House, 4/5 Amber Business Village, Amber Close, Amington, Tamworth, Staffordshire B77 4RP

Rising Stars UK Ltd.
22 Grafton Street, London W1S 4EX
www.risingstars-uk.com

First published 2006

Cover design: Button plc
Cover image: Alamy
Illustrator: Bill Greenhead
Text design and typesetting: Marmalade Book Design (www.marmaladebookdesign.com)
Educational consultants: Cliff Moon, Lorraine Petersen and Paul Blum
Technical consultant: Helen Nelson
Pictures: The Advertising Archives: pages 4-5, 14, 20, 21
Alamy: pages 6, 7, 9, 10-11, 26, 27, 30, 40, 41
Empics: pages 32, 33, 35, 42-43, 43
The Kobal Collection: pages 22, 23, 24, 25
AKG Images: pages 25, 46
Getty Images: 13, 30, 31

British Library Cataloguing in Publication Data.
A CIP record for this book is available from the British Library.

ISBN: 978-1-84680-043-6

Printed by Craftprint International Ltd., Singapore

Contents

Cool brands

Cool brands are the brands we all want.

Cool brands stand for taste and style.

They are also the brands that celebrities
and **style icons** choose to have.

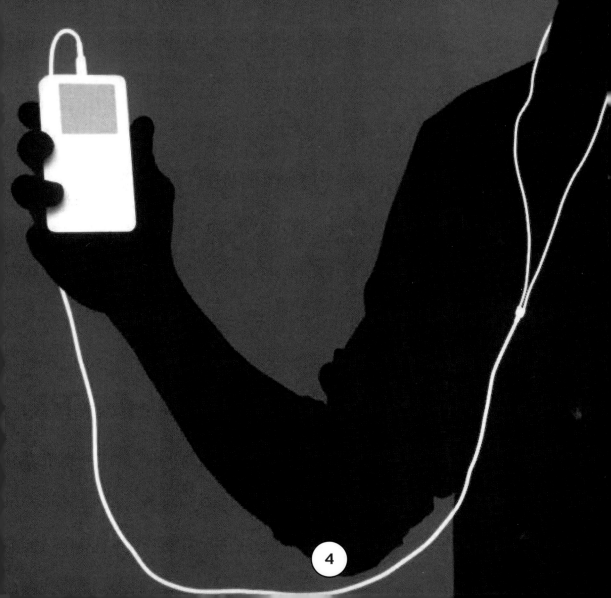

The Top Five Cool Factors!

Stylish	✔
Original	✔
Innovative	✔
Authentic	✔
Unique	✔

Superbrands

Less than 5% of all brands make the grade as cool brands!

The Council of Superbrands votes on the coolest brands each year.

These are some that they have chosen.

You can wear, drive, eat, read and play them!

Ducati has been voted
the coolest brand of motorcycle.

Coolest...	Brand
Watch	Tag Heuer
Sunglasses	Oakley
Clothes	Diesel
Music	The Streets
Car	Audi
Magazine	Dazed and Confused
Games	Sony PlayStation
Food	Häagen Dazs ice-cream

History of a brand: Coca-Cola

Some brands have kept their cool for over 100 years!

Coca-Cola began in 1886.

It was sold from a chemist's store in Atlanta USA and cost five cents a glass.

Today it is sold in 200 countries worldwide.

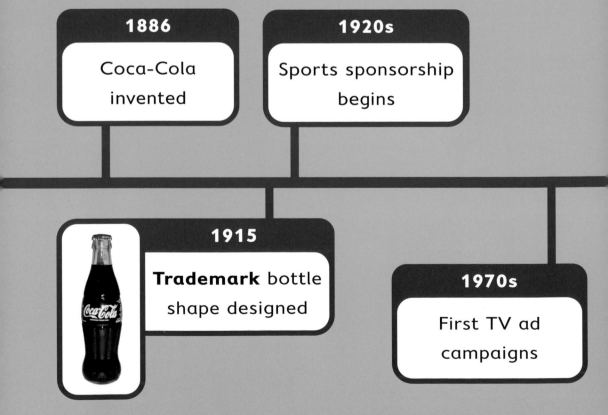

1886

Coca-Cola invented

1920s

Sports sponsorship begins

1915

Trademark bottle shape designed

1970s

First TV ad campaigns

1982

Diet Coke launched

2000

Coca-Cola is marketed in nearly 200 countries worldwide

Coca-Cola facts

Coca-Cola was the first soft drink in space in 1985.

Mycokemusic.com was one of the first legal music download sites.

The artist Andy Warhol used Coca-Cola in some of his Pop Art pictures.

Coca-Cola's **contour** bottle is easy to recognise — even in the dark!

Coca-Cola sponsors lots of cool sports events:

FIFA World Cup

Olympic Games

Rugby World Cup

UK Football League

Creating a brand

Expert teams work together to make a brand.

Marketing team –
promotes and sells product

Designer –
designs the product

What does the
team do?

Naming specialist –
thinks up brand name

Researcher –
finds out what's cool

Brand protection team –
makes sure brand isn't copied

Brands and brains

We use the right side of our brain to read brand names.

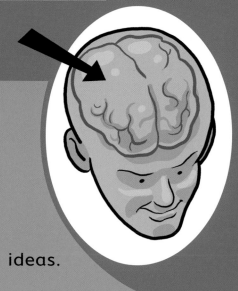

This means we respond with our emotions.

That's why brand names have power over us!

We link brands with images and ideas.

When we buy the brand, we are buying into a dream.

Marketing a brand

Brands are marketed on billboards, in magazines and on TV.

They use **logos** and slogans so that we recognise them instantly.

Slogan

Logo

Buzz marketing

'Buzz or 'sneeze' marketing spreads brand names like a virus.

It uses word of mouth to promote brands.

Companies give out free products for people to try. If people like the product they will talk about it.

Sometimes, companies pay people to talk about their brands!

Coolhunters

Cool keeps changing.

Coolhunters are 'culture spies'.

They are paid to spy on the teen market and spot cool trends.

How do they do it?

They carry out **surveys**.

They visit teens at home to ask them what's cool and what's not.

They go out into streets, schools and shopping malls to spot the style leaders. They ask the style leaders what they want, and why.

They hold teen **focus groups**.

A Nose for Cool
(Part one)

It was Jay's birthday.

He opened his present. It was a pair of trainers.

"Um ... thanks, Mum."

"What's wrong?" Mum said. "You said you wanted trainers."

"Yes ... they're great," Jay said. He wasn't a good actor.

"You said they were the coolest brand," Mum reminded him.

"They were … last Christmas!" Jay said.

"Oh, I can't keep up with this cool thing," Mum said.

"It's okay, Mum," Jay said. "Cool keeps changing, that's all."

"So what's the coolest now?" Mum asked.

"The ones with the MP3 link," Jay told her.

Mum looked blank.

"Tyler Price has a pair."

But then, Tyler always had the coolest brand.

"Well, I've got other things to worry about," Mum said. "Someone has stolen the raffle prizes from the church hall."

"Not that aftershave?" Jay said. "I wanted to win that!"

"Well, it's gone!" Mum said. "And we have to find the thief – or it may happen again."

Continued on page 28

Celebrities and brands

Some brands are cool because celebrities use them, advertise them or design them.

Stars like Missy Elliott and Madonna wear Gap clothes.

David Beckham isn't just a footballer — he's a **style icon**. People want to wear the same brands as he does.

Tracksuit top 19.99

Madonna became the face of H&M in 2006. She designed the tracksuit in this picture.

Films and brands

Films can make places and products cool.

Lord of the Rings: The Two Towers (2002)

Woody Allen's film **Manhattan** (1979) made
New York cool.

The **Lord of the Rings** movies did the same for
New Zealand.

Tourists flocked to Tokyo after seeing **Lost in
Translation** (2003).

Famous films can create new product brands.
Charlie and the Chocolate Factory (2005)
led to Wonka chocolate bars.

Charlie with a Wonka bar in a scene from the film.

Food fact!

Bertie Bott's Every
Flavour Beans are a
spin-off from the
Harry Potter films.

Product placement in films

Brands earn cool **status** when they are shown in films.

This is called product placement.

It works for any product, from food and drink to cars.

The Island (2005)
The character played by Scarlett Johansson watches an advert — for Scarlett Johansson's perfume!

X-Men: The Last Stand (2006) Cyclops puts on Oakley sunglasses and a Belstaff jacket and rides away on a Harley-Davidson motorcycle. Result: cool brand placement!

Cool product placements

BMW Z3	**GoldenEye** (1995)
Mr Potato Head	**Toy Story** (1995)
X-Box, Puma, MSN, Nokia, Calvin Klein	**The Island** (2005)

Check out these 'fairy tale brands' in **Shrek 2** (2004).

- Versachery
- Farbucks coffee
- Burger Prince!

Cool venues

Even museums can be cool.

The Guardian newspaper called
the Design Museum in London the 'Temple of Cool'.

It has been voted one of the UK's five
coolest venues.

Why is the Design Museum cool?

✔ Shows the work of young designers.

✔ Holds workshops run by top designers.

✔ Has interactive
exhibitions.

✔ Presents awards
for design.

Another cool UK venue is the London Eye.

It has become the coolest new landmark on the London skyline.

Why is the London Eye cool?

✔ The biggest observation wheel in the world.

✔ Venue for parties, weddings and **product launches**.

✔ Major tourist attraction.

✔ Popular website link.

A Nose for Cool
(Part two)

The next day, Tyler was showing off his watch.
It was the coolest brand, of course.

"Very nice," Jay said. "Those trainers are great,
too."

"These? Yeah. No-one else has got them yet,"
Tyler boasted.

Then Jay smelt something. He recognised that
smell. Surely it was ...?

"What's up?" Tyler asked.

"Nothing!' Jay said. But he had a plan.

Later on, he asked Mum about the stuff that had gone from the church hall.

"What kind of stuff went missing?" he asked.

"Let me think – not the girl's stuff, though there was some nice make-up." Mum said.

"But the aftershave, and the computer data stick and things like that?" asked Jay.

"Yes, it was all top stuff!" Mum said.
"Even some cool brands!" She winked.

Continued on page 34

Nokia – hi-tech cool

Nokia is a global leader in hi-tech goods.

Nokia used to make paper, card, rubber tyres, boots and raincoats!

Then came mobile phones.

The first 'mobile' had a 10 kg charging box. It was as big as a suitcase!

Today's Nokia phones tick these cool boxes:

Innovation

 First texting

 First Internet access

 First cameras

Style

- ☑ First changeable covers
- ☑ Fashion collection based on catwalk trends

Sponsors

- ☑ X-Factor
- ☑ London Fashion Week
- ☑ Urban sports like **Streetball** and **Parkour**

Hummer

Hummer is an American company. It makes world-famous **SUVs**.

The **SUVs** began as military vehicles. These were used in '**Desert Storm**' in the 1990s.

Hummer **SUVs** are called Humvees.

HUMMER

A Humvee featured in the
movie **Stormbreaker** (2006).

H1 Alpha factfile:

Brand values:

- Freedom

- Strength

- **Authenticity**

Performance:

It can:

- climb a 55° vertical wall

- scale a 60% gradient

- drive in 76 cm of water.

Marketing:

- The H1 Alpha is in hip-hop videos and blockbuster movies.

- It is driven by celebrities.

- Adverts for the H1 Alpha have won awards.

- There are Hummer branded clothes, equipment and toys.

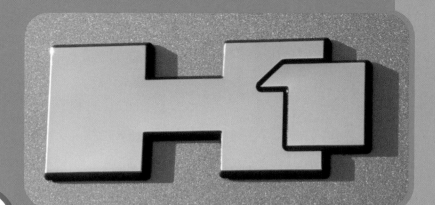

Aluminium rustproof body

Tyres that can run flat

Chrome grille

A Nose for Cool
(Part three)

Later on, Jay went to the church hall with Mum. The window at the side was open. They went inside.

"Oh, no!" Mum said. 'It looks like the thief's been back!"

Jay went outside. He pushed past the bushes to the window. He sniffed. There was that smell again! It was that prize aftershave, he was sure. Then he saw a footprint just under the window. He called to Mum.

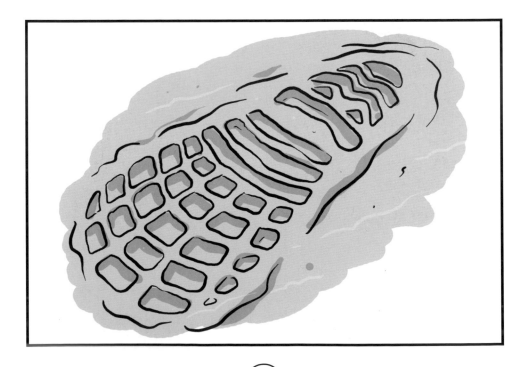

"Mum, I know who the thief is!' said Jay.

"You do? But how?"

"That footprint!" Jay pointed it out.
"There's only one trainer that makes a print like that. And there's only one person with those trainers!"

Continued on the next page

The police called at Tyler's house later that day. His room was full of stuff from the church raffle. It still had the raffle numbers on! The church sale got everything back ... even the aftershave. Tyler had to go down to the police station with Mum.

"The vicar wants you to have this as a reward, Jay!" Mum said. She gave him the aftershave.

"Really? Mint!" Jay said.

At least he would smell cool now! After all, he had a nose for it!

PlayStation

PlayStation is one of Sony's cool brands.

Sony took gaming to a new adult market.

PlayStation's slogan is: 'Don't underestimate the power of PlayStation.'

✔ Powerful technology

✔ Cool styling

✔ Lifestyle branding

PlayStation keeps gamers interested.

Shaping **symbols** – insiders knew what they meant. Everyone else wanted to know!

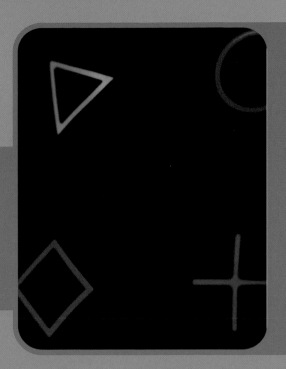

The PSP – now you could play anywhere.

PlayStation Experience parties – these proved that gamers do have friends!

MTV

MTV is one of the world's top brands.

It works hard to keep ahead of the youth market.

Focus groups

One-to-one home interviews with teens

How does MTV keep its cool?

Interactive technology – viewers can phone in, text, fax and email

MUSIC TE

MTV now reaches 407 million viewers in over 160 countries! It hosts awards shows for movies, music and music videos every year.

Robbie Williams won an MTV award for music in 2005.

Quiz

1   Name three of the top five cool factors.

2   What is the percentage of 'cool' brands?

3   Which brand was voted the coolest clothing brand?

4   Which artist used Coca-Cola in his works?

5   What **does** Nike use as its logo?

6   **What is 'buzz' ma**rketing?

7   **Name two places** made cool by movies.

8   **What does produ**ct placement mean?

9   **Which building** in London has been called the Temple **of Cool?**

10 Name two things that make Nokia an innovative brand.

Glossary of terms

authentic	The real thing.
contour	The shape or outline of something.
Desert Storm	A military operation by the United States and Allies to free Kuwait from Iraq.
focus groups	Groups of people who are interviewed to gather their views.
innovative	New and fresh.
interactive technology	Links through computers that let you choose what you view and change it.
logos	Names, symbols or trademarks.
Parkour	An extreme sport of running and jumping through cities.
product launches	Events held to show a new product to the public.
status	Position or ranking, compared with others.
Streetball	A kind of basketball played in cities.
style icons	People who are famous for their fashion style – other people copy them.
surveys	Reports based on interviews with large numbers of people.
SUV	A four-wheel drive Sports Utility Vehicle.
symbol	A picture that stands for something else.
trademark	A brand that is protected by laws.
unique	One of a kind.

More resources

Books

Advertising (Behind the Media) by Catherine Chambers
Heinemann Library
ISBN: 0431114501
Lots of information on how products are made and marketed.

Advertising (Mediawise Series) by Julian Petley
Hodder Wayland
ISBN: 0750240504
How and why adverts are made, with job profiles and other inside info.

Magazines

GQ Style
Men's magazine on looking good, new trends and designer brands.

Websites

www.superbrands.org
The website of the Superbrands organisation packed with information and case studies of cool brands, sports brands and kids' superbrands.

www.teentoday.co.uk
Website for teens with features on new trends, products and celebrity styles.

www.bbc.co.uk/teens
The BBC website for teens.

Video/DVD

Shrek 2 (2004)
Cat. no. B0002VE5GW
Look out for the many references to famous brands, pop icons, the movies and fast-food chains.

Answers

1 Any three of style, innovation, authentic, unique, original.

2 5%

3 Diesel

4 Andy Warhol

5 A 'swoosh' symbol.

6 Promoting a brand by word of mouth.

7 Any two of New Zealand, Manhattan, Tokyo.

8 Showing a product in a movie to promote it.

9 The Design Museum

10 Any two of first texting, cameras or Internet access.

Index